ASA-SP-10
ISBN 978-1-56027-653-1

Printed in the United States of America

Aviation Supplies & Academics, Inc.
7005 132nd Place SE
Newcastle, Washington 98059-3153
Email: asa@asa2fly.com
Website: www.asa2fly.com

[03]24

Name____

Mailing Address____________________________________

____

____

Phone _________________________ Email________________________________

Logbook Number___________ ____ Date of Issue _______________________

From _________________________ To _______________________

YEAR 20___ DATE	AIRCRAFT MAKE & MODEL	AIRCRAFT IDENT.	POINTS OF DEPARTURE & ARRIVAL		AIRCRAFT CATEGORY				TYPE OF PILOTING TIME					
			FROM	TO		AIRPLANE SEL			DUAL RECEIVED		PILOT-IN-COMMAND		CROSS-COUNTRY	
PAGE TOTAL														
AMOUNT FORWARD														
TOTAL TO DATE														

| GROUND TRAINER | CONDITIONS OF FLIGHT | | | | | | NO. LDG. | | TOTAL DURATION OF FLIGHT | | REMARKS, PROCEDURES, MANEUVERS |
	DAY		NIGHT		SIMULATED INSTRUMENT		DAY	NIGHT			
											I certify that the statements made by me on this form are true.

PILOT'S SIGNATURE

YEAR 20___	AIRCRAFT MAKE & MODEL	AIRCRAFT IDENT.	POINTS OF DEPARTURE & ARRIVAL		AIRCRAFT CATEGORY			TYPE OF PILOTING TIME		
DATE			FROM	TO		AIRPLANE SEL		DUAL RECEIVED	PILOT-IN-COMMAND	CROSS-COUNTRY
PAGE TOTAL										
AMOUNT FORWARD										
TOTAL TO DATE										

GROUND TRAINER		CONDITIONS OF FLIGHT						NO. LDG.		TOTAL DURATION OF FLIGHT		REMARKS, PROCEDURES, MANEUVERS
		DAY		NIGHT		SIMULATED INSTRUMENT		DAY	NIGHT			
												I certify that the statements made by me on this form are true.

PILOT'S SIGNATURE

YEAR 20___ DATE	AIRCRAFT MAKE & MODEL	AIRCRAFT IDENT.	POINTS OF DEPARTURE & ARRIVAL		AIRCRAFT CATEGORY				TYPE OF PILOTING TIME		
			FROM	TO		AIRPLANE SEL			DUAL RECEIVED	PILOT-IN-COMMAND	CROSS-COUNTRY
PAGE TOTAL											
AMOUNT FORWARD											
TOTAL TO DATE											

| GROUND TRAINER | | CONDITIONS OF FLIGHT | | | NO. LDG. | | TOTAL DURATION OF FLIGHT | | REMARKS, PROCEDURES, MANEUVERS |
		DAY	NIGHT	SIMULATED INSTRUMENT	DAY	NIGHT			

I certify that the statements made by me on this form are true.

PILOT'S SIGNATURE

YEAR 20___ DATE	AIRCRAFT MAKE & MODEL	AIRCRAFT IDENT.	POINTS OF DEPARTURE & ARRIVAL		AIRCRAFT CATEGORY			TYPE OF PILOTING TIME		
			FROM	TO	AIRPLANE SEL			DUAL RECEIVED	PILOT-IN-COMMAND	CROSS-COUNTRY
			PAGE TOTAL							
			AMOUNT FORWARD							
			TOTAL TO DATE							

GROUND TRAINER		CONDITIONS OF FLIGHT					NO. LDG.		TOTAL DURATION OF FLIGHT		REMARKS, PROCEDURES, MANEUVERS
		DAY		NIGHT		SIMULATED INSTRUMENT		DAY / NIGHT				

I certify that the statements made by me on this form are true.

PILOT'S SIGNATURE

GROUND INSTRUCTION LOG

DATE	LESSON PLAN	INSTRUCTOR	TIME	RUNNING TOTAL

GROUND INSTRUCTION LOG

DATE	LESSON PLAN	INSTRUCTOR	TIME	RUNNING TOTAL

<table>
<tr><td>

PRE-SOLO ENDORSEMENTS
SOLO FLIGHT (FIRST 90-DAY)

</td><td>

CROSS-COUNTRY FLIGHT TRAINING
CROSS COUNTRY SOLO FLIGHT

</td></tr>
<tr><td>

I certify that Mr./Ms. _______________
has satisfactorily completed the presolo knowledge exam of §61.87(b), received the pre-solo training required by §61.87 in a

(make and model) _______________,

and has demonstrated satisfactory proficiency and safety on the maneuvers and procedures required by §61.87 in this or similar make and model of aircraft to be flown.

SIGNED _______________ DATE _______________

CFI NO. _______________ EXPIRATION DATE _______________

</td><td>

I certify that Mr./Ms. _______________
has received the required solo cross-country training and find he/she has met the applicable requirements of §61.93, and is proficient to make solo cross-country

flights in a *(make and model aircraft)* _______________.

SIGNED _______________ DATE _______________

CFI NO. _______________ EXPIRATION DATE _______________

</td></tr>
<tr><td>

I certify that Mr./Ms. _______________
has received the required training to qualify for solo flying. I have determined he/she meets the applicable requirements of §61.87(n) and is proficient to make solo flights in

(make and model) _______________.

SIGNED _______________ DATE _______________

CFI NO. _______________ EXPIRATION DATE _______________

</td><td>

I have reviewed the preflight planning and preparation of Mr./Ms. _______________
_______________ and find that he/she is prepared to make the solo flight safely under the known circumstances from _______________

airport to _______________ airport via _______________

with landings at _______________ airport(s) in a _______________

on this date, subject to the following conditions: _______________

SIGNED _______________ DATE _______________

CFI NO. _______________ EXPIRATION DATE _______________

</td></tr>
</table>

ADDITIONAL AIRPORT SOLO FLIGHT NIGHT SOLO FLIGHT	SOLO FLIGHT (ADDITIONAL 90-DAY) TSA U.S. CITIZENSHIP
I certify that Mr./Ms. __________ has received the required training of § 61.93(b)(1). I have determined that he/she is proficient to practice solo takeoffs and landings at *(airport name)* __________ __________ subject to the following conditions: __________. SIGNED __________ DATE __________ CFI NO. __________ EXPIRATION DATE __________	I certify that Mr./Ms. __________ has received the required training to qualify for solo flying. I have determined that he/she meets the applicable requirements of §61.87(p) and is proficient to make solo flights in (make and model) __________. SIGNED __________ DATE __________ CFI NO. __________ EXPIRATION DATE __________
I certify that Mr./Ms. __________ has received the required pre-solo training in a *(make and model aircraft)* __________, #__________. I have determined he/she has demonstrated the proficiency of §61.87(o) and is proficient to make solo flights at night in that make and model aircraft. SIGNED __________ DATE __________ CFI NO. __________ EXPIRATION DATE __________	I certify that Mr./Ms. __________ has presented me a (type of document presented and the relevant control or se- quential number on the document, if any)__________, #__________, establishing that he/she is a U.S. citizen or national in accordance with 49 CFR § 1552.3(h). SIGNED __________ DATE __________ CFI NO. __________ EXPIRATION DATE __________

AIRCRAFT FLOWN AND NUMBER OF HOURS IN EACH

AIRCRAFT MAKE AND MODEL	PIC	DUAL	AIRCRAFT MAKE AND MODEL	PIC	DUAL

NOTES

NOTES